box frame.
magic

Lizzie O'Prey
with Helen Atkinson

David & Charles

A DAVID & CHARLES BOOK

First published in the UK in 2003

Copyright © Lizzie O'Prey 2003

Distributed in North America
by F&W Publications Inc
4700 E Galbraith Road
Cincinnati OH 45236
1-800-289-0963

A catalogue record for this book is available from the British Library.

ISBN 0 7153 1496 3 hardback
ISBN 0 7153 1497 1 paperback (USA only)

Printed in Great Britain by Butler & Tanner, Frome, Somerset
for David & Charles
Brunel House, Newton Abbot, Devon

commissioning editor Fiona Eaton
desk editor Jennifer Proverbs
executive art editor Ali Myer
senior designer Prudence Rogers
production controller Jennifer Campbell

Visit our website at www.davidandcharles.co.uk

David & Charles books are available from all good bookshops; alternatively you can contact our
Orderline on (0)1626 334555 or write to us at FREEPOST EX2 110, David & Charles *Direct*,
Newton Abbot, TQ12 4ZZ (no stamp required UK mainland).

The author and publisher have made every effort to ensure that all the instructions in this book
are accurate and safe, and therefore cannot accept liability for any resulting injury, damage
or loss to persons or property however it may arise.

contents

introduction	4
materials and equipment	6
making box frames	8
finishing your frames	14
natural style	16
fresh and wild	18
garden source	24
floral bounty	28
countrywide	32
designs on nature	36
family occasions	38
holiday memories	40
wedding bells	44
hello baby	48
weekend break	52
celebrating special moments	56
classic displays	58
home sweet home	60
treasure trove	66
sewing matters	70
simple style	74
collecting memories	78
making art	80
picture this	82
modern image	88
candy art	92
fine design	96
the latest looks	100
suppliers	102
index	104

introduction

From portraits and pictures to photographs and fine maps, the array of images that you can put on show all have one thing in common – they rely on a carefully chosen setting. Traditionally this has been a flat finished frame – but with more and more diverse items to display, this basic design no longer fulfils every requirement, and the box frame (also known as a shadow box) has evolved to show off more unusual exhibits. This book is all about taking some well-known skills and bringing them bang up-to-date with easy instructions for making a variety of box frames and a selection of innovative ideas for what to display in them.

The first section of this book equips you with the simple skills and techniques you need to make a variety of box frames, then the projects explore the myriad of materials that can be used to make a perfect box frame display. It may be flowers that fill a frame, a message to a loved one or a collection of memories from a special moment that you want to put in the picture.

We have tried to offer a range of projects with different skill levels throughout, with plenty of alternative ideas for what to display and how and where to hang your frame. Whatever your passion, a stylish box frame can provide the creative solution.

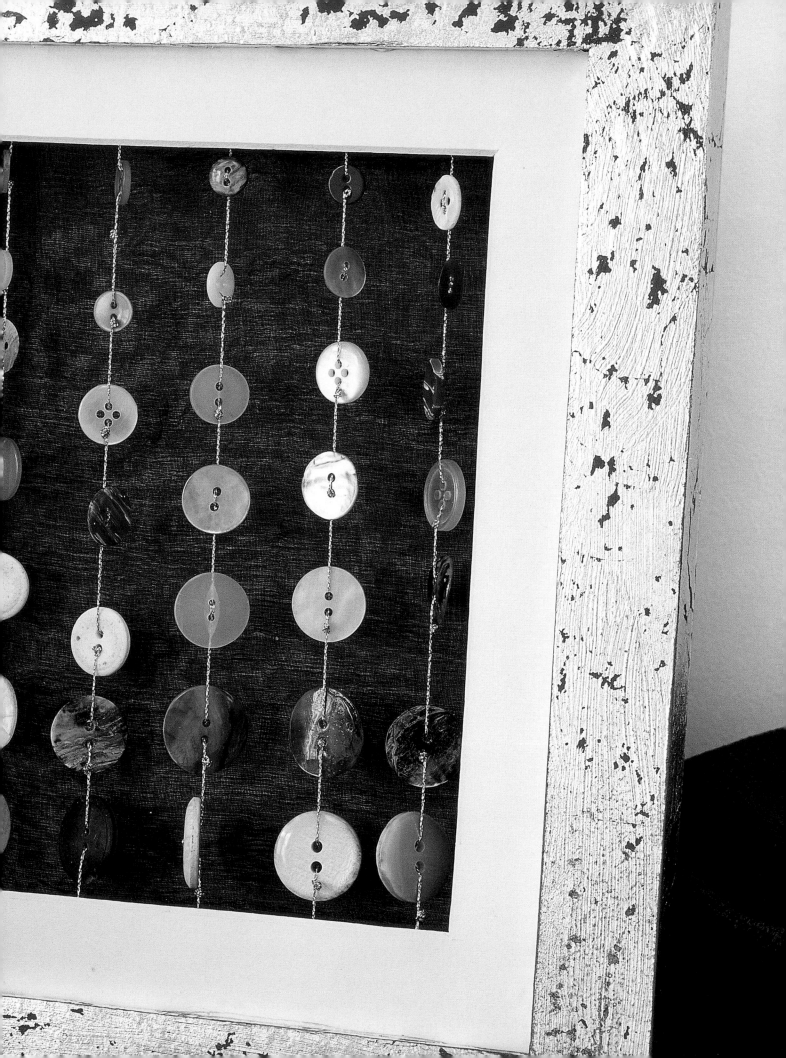

materials & equipment

With any project-based book, you are often faced with a list of 'must haves', 'buy this' and 'you'll need plenty of these'. However, it's best to read through some of the projects before you start, and then decide on the materials and equipment you require. If you decide to make a simple surround such as the one used for Sewing Matters (see page 70) your shopping list will be shorter than if you tackle the more decorative box frame made for Hello Baby (see page 48). Start simple, acquire your materials and equipment one project at a time and you'll enjoy making box frames as you learn each new skill.

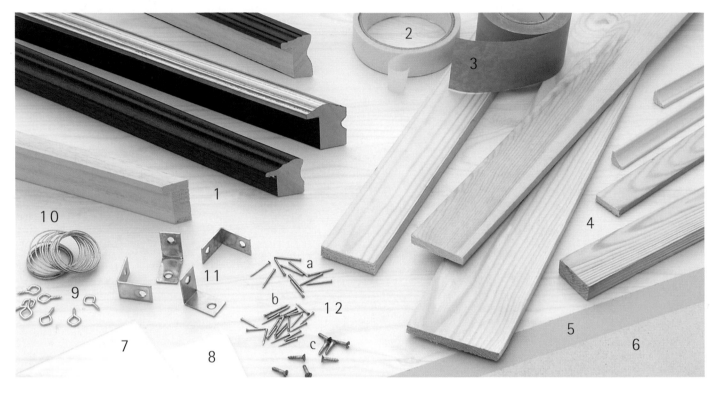

MATERIALS

1 **Wood mouldings** Use to create your frame for a ready-made finish. For the best selection visit a specialist framers or look on-line for mail order mouldings. Also try do-it-yourself (DIY) shops and timber merchants.

2 **Masking tape** Secures glued surrounds and finished projects. A handy quick fix but not as strong as brown paper tape.

3 **Brown paper tape** Use ready-gummed types for finishing frames. This creates a total seal and will prevent moisture getting in.

4 **Wood** Throughout the book you'll see how different shapes, sizes and lengths can be adapted to make your box frame. Before you start any project decide on the style and this will help you choose your wood. Slim pieces, roughly 2cm (¾in) wide, will suit a delicate subject and will work for a box frame that is not too deep, roughly 3–4cm (1¼–1¾in).

Chunkier wood, roughly 3cm (1¼in) wide, will suit a bulkier project and deeper box. Medium density fibreboard (mdf) has a smooth, non-porous finish. Work outside when cutting mdf and always wear a face-mask.

5 **Mountboard** Available in a range of colours. Use to make a picture mount that creates a 'frame within a frame'. You'll find a choice of black or white plus green and a variety of patterns. Buy this as you need it as an art shop will store it keeping it flat and dry – once it warps it is useless. If you can't find the colour you want, you cover a white mount with your own choice of paper.

6 **Backing board** Self-explanatory! It's what you use to make the back of the frame.

7 **Glass** It is not always necessary to use glass in a box frame – if you do decide to use it have it cut by a professional glazier.

8 **Perspex** Can be used as an alternative front or back to your frame.

9 **Eyehooks** Useful for suspending items in your frame.

10 **Wire** Use to suspend objects in the box frame, or to hang the frame itself when you put it on display. Make sure you use proper picture wire when hanging heavy frames. You'll find it at specialist frame suppliers or picture framers. If your box frame project is very light you can choose nylon cord to hang the frame – this is widely available from haberdashery departments of department stores.

11 **L Brackets** Secure your finished frame with these handy brackets.

12 a, b, c **Panel pins, nails and screws** Used for putting the frame together, finishing and hanging.

EQUIPMENT

1 Wood adhesive Use to stick pieces of your frame together.

2 Glue gun A sturdy option when making the surround. The gun is plugged into the electricity mains and the glue heats up gradually – use the glue when it is slightly runny. Take care – hot glue burns.

3 Sandpaper Neaten edges and smooth down joints. Choose a medium grade when working on really rough joints or lengths of wood and a fine grade when preparing pieces for paint effects or simple staining.

4 Mitre saw Invest in one of these if you are planning on making a lot of frames. It cuts the corners neatly. Available from DIY shops or builders' merchants.

5 Jigsaw For cutting out windows from solid pieces of wood. Available from DIY shops or builders' merchants.

6 Mitre block An inexpensive alternative to a mitre saw which enables you to cut straight lines and 45-degree angles for corners. Available from do-it-yourself shops or builders' merchants.

7 Cutting mat A protective surface when working with any kind of cutting device. They come in a range of different sizes and if you are planning on doing a lot of frame work then buy a really decent size. You'll find them in any good art shop.

8 Pencil Essential for marking measurements.

9 Ruler Yes sometimes it's the millimetres that count! Use a metal ruler as an edge to cut against with a craft knife.

10 Scissors Vital for any frame, to make clean cuts and finish edges.

11 Craft knives Use on the cutting mat for trimming paper and cutting clean lines.

12 Hammer Needed to work with panel pins and nails.

13 Tenon saw A companion tool to your mitre block. Available from DIY shops or builders' merchants.

14 Corner clamp Use to secure joints while the glue sets.

15 Drill Have a variety of bits available so that you can make different size holes as required.

16 Bradawl When you need to put in a screw it is often better to make the initial hole with one of these.

making box frames

There are three basic elements of a box frame: the frame back, the box frame – in which the objects are displayed – and the frame surround, which provides the decorative finish. To these you can add decorative paper or fabric to cover the frame back, a picture mount and glass if required.

In this section you'll find four simple methods for making a box frame, instructions for cutting a picture mount and a guide to assembling the completed box frame – putting together the frame back, the box frame and the frame surround. Remember that any one of these techniques can be adapted to suit your own needs and you can mix and match different elements of each. Decide on the dimensions of your box frame before you begin to build it, taking into account what you want to fill it with and the type of display you want to create. (For more information on what wood to use see Materials, page 6.)

METHOD A

This is a simple approach to making your frame, and a perfect choice for a first time framer.

materials and equipment

glass (optional)
backing board
ruler
pencil
cutting mat
craft knife
planed soft wood
mitre block
tenon saw
wood adhesive
hammer
panel pins
masking tape

To Make the Frame Back

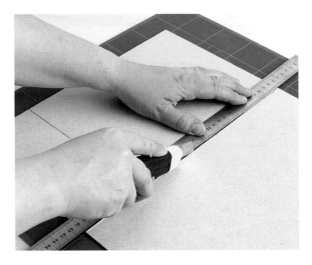

◄ step one

Decide on the size of your box frame and mark out the height and width on your backing board. If you already have a piece of glass, it's often easier to cut the backing board to the same dimensions – if not then make your frame and take it to a glazier to cut the finished piece of glass. Score along the lines several times with a craft knife.

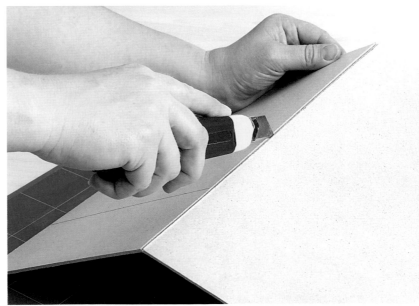

▲ step two

Bend the board back along the scored lines and cut down the open edge.

To Make the Box Frame

▲ step one

Measure and mark two pieces of wood the length of the backing board minus the depth of the wood and two pieces the width of the backing board minus the depth of the wood. Cut the wood to the marked lengths. This is the basis for the box frame.

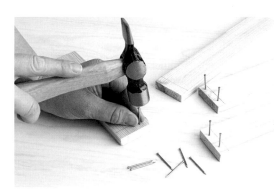

▲ step two

Mark off the depth of the wood on one end of each piece. Lightly tap in two panel pins about 1.5–3mm (¹⁄₁₆–¹⁄₈in) in at each marked end.

▲ step three

Apply wood adhesive to the end of each piece of wood and assemble the box frame.

▲ step four

Tap in the panel pins with the hammer and leave overnight to dry. This is the box part of the frame.

To Make the Frame Surround

Measure and mark two pieces of wood the length of the backing board minus the width of the wood, and two pieces the width of the backing board minus the width of the wood. Cut the wood. On a flat surface, glue the four pieces together to make a frame. Secure with masking tape and leave overnight to dry.

METHOD B

B

This is a more advanced way of making your frame. The mitred corners are more in keeping with traditional looks for frame surrounds.

materials and equipment

glass (optional)
backing board
ruler
pencil
cutting mat
craft knife
wood
mitre block
tenon saw
wood adhesive
masking tape

To Make the Frame Back

Follow method A, page 8.

To Make the Box Frame

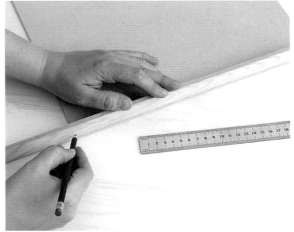

▲ step one

Mitre one end of a length of wood, roughly the width of your frame back.

▲ step two

Hold the mitred piece against the frame back and make a 45-degree angle mark at the width of the frame back at the uncut end. Mitre this end and then cut and mitre another three pieces to create the box frame. Glue each joint, secure with masking tape and leave overnight to dry.

To Make the Frame Surround

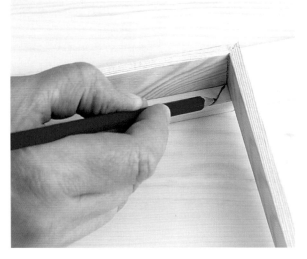

▲ step one

Mitre one end of a piece of wood. Position the box frame on top of the mitred wood allowing approximately a 1cm (⅜in) return inside so that the mitred join on the box frame lines up with the mitred end of the piece of wood.

▲ step two

At the opposite end of the piece of wood, draw a line into the corner of the box. This marks where you make your next mitred cut. Continue until you have four pieces. On a flat surface, glue the four pieces together, secure with masking tape and leave overnight to dry.

METHOD C

Using wood mouldings you can take a short cut and create a box and surround in one.

materials and equipment

glass
backing board
ruler
pencil
cutting mat
craft knife
wood moulding
mitre saw
wood adhesive
masking tape

To Make the Frame Back

Follow method A, page 8.

To Make the Box Frame and Surround

C

 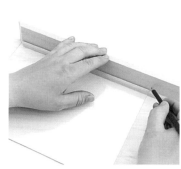 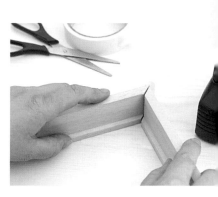

▲ step one

Mitre one end of a length of wood moulding, roughly the width of your glass.

▲ step two

Hold the mitred piece against the glass and, allowing 1.5mm ($\frac{1}{16}$in) extra, mark vertically where the next mitred cut will be. This will allow you to insert the glass with ease. Continue until you have four pieces for your frame.

▲ step three

Glue each joint, secure with masking tape and leave overnight to dry.

METHOD D

Another alternative for the frame surround is to cut a whole piece from a square of mdf. This gives you a frame front with no joins and is perfect for modern style images.

materials and equipment

piece of mdf
ruler
pencil
face mask
blocks of wood
drill
jigsaw
sandpaper

TIP

Work outside when cutting mdf and always wear a face-mask.

To Make the Frame Back and Box Frame

Follow method A or B, pages 8–10.

To Make the Frame Surround

D

▲ step one

Measure the dimensions of the outside of the box frame and cut a piece of mdf to this size plus 5cm (2in) all round. Measure in 6cm (2½in) from the edge of the mdf and draw a rectangle on the mdf.

▲ step two

Place the mdf on top of blocks of wood and drill a hole at each corner of the rectangle. This allows you to insert the jigsaw blade.

▲ step three

Insert the jigsaw blade into the first hole and cut in a straight line down one full side. Remove jigsaw, turn mdf, put jigsaw in the next hole and repeat. Continue until you have cut out the central panel. Sand all edges to give a smooth finish.

CUTTING A PICTURE MOUNT

Adding a mount to your frame complements the finished piece. They aren't always necessary, more modern pieces may not require one, but you can add them as and when you want a more traditional finish.

materials and equipment

mountboard
picture glass
pencil
cutting mat
ruler
craft knife

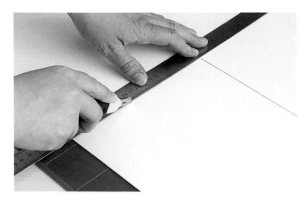

▲ **step one**

Place your glass on the mountboard and draw around it. Using the ruler and craft knife cut out the mountboard to this size.

◄ **step two**

Measure in an equal distance all the way around. (Depending on the size of your frame surround 3–4cm (1¼–1¾in) is a good guide.) Draw a rectangle, then cut it out to make a window – this is your mount.

TIP

If you are feeling confident and want a really professional finish, angle the craft knife blade at 45 degrees towards the middle of the mount as you cut to give an angled finish. Remember to keep a steady hand and apply a firm, even pressure as you cut in one smooth go.

ASSEMBLING THE FRAME

There are many different ways to put your frame together, and once you have made a few you may find and perfect your own individual technique.

In the meantime, here are three methods to get you started: assembling open-fronted frames, assembling frames with a glass and a mount, and assembling frames with a rebated surround.

Open-Fronted Frames

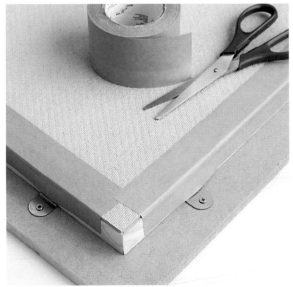

▲ **step one**

Centre the box frame on the frame surround and secure using brackets.

▲ **step two**

Place the frame back on the box frame and secure with brown paper tape.

Frames With Glass and a Mount

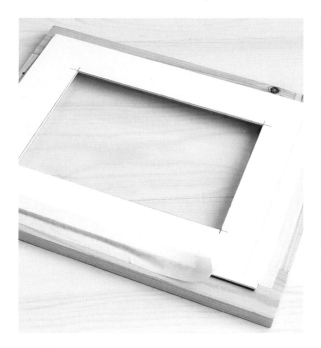

▲ step one

Centre the glass on top of the frame surround. Place the mount on top and secure with masking tape.

▲ step two

Panel pin the box frame to the frame back.

▲ step three

Place the box frame on top of the assembled surround. Place lengths of moulding along each side of the box and panel pin in position to secure.

Frames With a Rebated Surround

▲ step one

Place glass inside frame surround and panel pin around the inside to hold the glass in place.

◄ step two

Glue gun the frame back to the box frame.

finishing your frames

There are an endless variety of paint colours, stains, varnishes and techniques that you can use to complete the look of your frames. It's important to consider the contents of the frame when choosing this final part of any project. Where bold colours make up part of the image a contrasting colour may make the most impact, but where you have used more subtle shades or tones, an aged or broken paint effect in matching shades is often the better choice.

Consider the overall colour scheme in the room in which you intend to display the piece. If your design has a white back and neutral surround, placing it against a dark colour will make the images stand out. Alternatively boldly coloured pieces will benefit from being hung against a white or neutral coloured background.

EMULSIONS AND ACRYLICS

Plain emulsion or acrylic paint are fine if you are looking to achieve a flat, one-colour finish for your piece. Small tester pots, available from decorating or DIY shops usually have enough for you to finish a frame, and because they are so inexpensive, you can afford to keep a wide selection in store. You'll find acrylic paints in craft shops and these can be easily tinted with white to create your own chosen shade.

STAINS AND VARNISHES

Although you can now find wood stains and varnishes in a myriad of colours from purples and pinks to blues and greens, these are more traditionally in natural and neutral wood tones and make the perfect choice for projects that use collections garnered from nature including seed heads and leaves. While available in both water and spirit-based formulas, you'll find the water-based options much more pleasant to work with. And the brushes are more easily cleaned afterwards. As an alternative to these, you can use water-based fabric dyes, or even damp tea bags dabbed on the surface of untreated light-wood will impart a little natural colour to your frame.

PAINT EFFECTS

Broken paint effects always give a wonderfully aged look to wood. One of the easiest of these techniques uses two colours of emulsion and a wax candle. Simply paint on a base colour and leave to dry. Then rub over the surface concentrating on the edges (or mouldings) with the candle and paint on a topcoat. Finally rub down your frame with sandpaper. Where the wax has adhered to the wood the top layer of paint will come away revealing layers of colour from beneath. This is a brilliantly simple project for children to try out. Another alternative to this is to use crackle glaze, which you'll find in any good craft or DIY shop.

ADDED EXTRAS

Metal leaf or metallic colours offer a rich alternative to a painted finish for your frame. Both are simple to use but both need to be applied with care. Make sure, if you are going to add gold or silver leaf to your frame, that you have a supply of soft brushes to hand with which to apply the leaf. And if you choose to use metallic paint, use an aerosol – it's so quick. But remember to work outside or in a well-ventilated area and wear a face-mask while you work.

natural style

Nature inspires us with its colours, textures and amazing designs. As an inspiration for making your own displays, there is encouragement wherever you look. Take a walk in the country and whether it is a curvy seed head or sea shell, a decorative leaf or feather, a berry or a cornflower in a field, you'll see something which will inspire. There's an amazing choice of natural shapes to collect or mould, cut and rearrange – every one perfect for the three-dimensional display that you can create in a box frame.

When you are deciding on where to display these natural collections think about the size of your frame in relation to the surrounding area. A tiny picture hung on the middle of a large blank wall will disappear, it is better placed in a small room or as part of a group of small images. A big frame will benefit from rooms with broad wall spaces, where they can dominate.

fresh and wild

Hand-cast hot chillies make a bright and unusual display when grouped together. This simple and stylish framed design could be hung in the kitchen, and would make a very fitting gift for a keen cook.

materials and equipment

silicone moulding paste
one fresh chilli
cutting mat
scalpel
plaster
small bowl
plastic teaspoon
red and green acrylic paints
small artist's paintbrush
clear acrylic varnish
box frame (see method A, pages 8–9)
white paper
aerosol glue
wood stain
absorbent paper or cloth
glue gun
picture mount (see page 12)

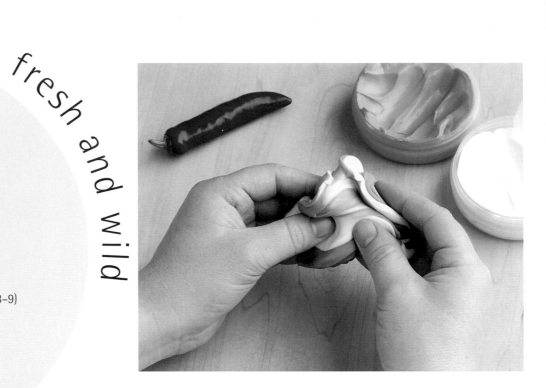

▲ step one

Take two walnut-sized balls of silicone moulding paste, one of each colour paste, and work them together until completely mixed.

step two ▶

Holding the chilli in one hand, mould the paste around the chilli leaving a small gap as you bring the two sides together. Make sure that the paste is an even thickness all over and no thinner than 6mm (¼in). Check that it fits snugly to the shape then leave for 5–10 minutes for the silicone moulding paste to set.

◄ step three

Using the scalpel carefully cut down one long edge of the mould. Only remove as much as you need to be able to pull out the chilli. Gradually cut away small slithers until you can access the chilli rather than taking away big chunks. Carefully remove the chilli from the mould.

step four ▶

Mix a small bowl of plaster to a creamy
consistency and using the teaspoon,
fill the mould. Leave to dry.

TIP

Treat the mould with care and
store it somewhere cool and dry.
This way, you should be able to
use it time and time again
to make plaster replicas.

▲ step five

Carefully remove the plaster chilli
from the mould and repeat steps 1–5
twice more, or use the same mould.

step six ▶

Paint the three plaster chillies, using
red acrylic paint for the chilli and
green for the stalk. Leave to dry.

▼ step seven

Using a clean, dry paintbrush, varnish the chillies all over to give them a shiny finish. Leave to dry.

▲ step eight

Cut the white paper to the same size as the backing board. Spray the backing board with glue and fix the backing paper in place.

step nine ▶

Colour the frame surround by rubbing over the surface with a cloth or absorbent paper soaked in a little wood stain. Work the colour in well to give a nicely aged appearance to the finished piece.

step ten ▶
Use the glue gun to stick the chillies in position on the backing paper. Remember that the glue gun can take 5–10 minutes to warm up.

◀ step eleven
Assemble the box frame (see pages 12-13). To avoid your display collecting dust or grease, you can always use frame glass cut to fit when assembling the box frame.

garden source

Seed heads are one of
nature's prettiest resources.
You'll find them in florists
and some department
stores, or gather your
own from the garden and
dry them in the airing
cupboard. Poppy heads are
used here, but star anise or
similar seed heads would
be equally effective.

garden source

materials and equipment

clear Perspex
cutting mat
ruler
strong craft knife
two sheets of handmade paper in
  different colours
poppy heads
aerosol glue
glue gun
box frame (see method C, page 11)
emulsion paint in two colours
small paintbrush
water-based crackle glaze
wax or clear varnish
frame glass cut to fit

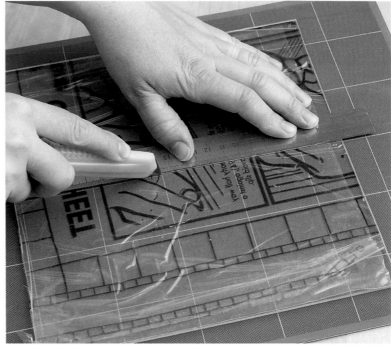

▲ step one

Cut the Perspex to size to make the frame back.

▲ step two

Tear a rectangle out of one of the coloured papers roughly 2cm (¾in)
smaller all round than the frame back. Tear another rectangle out of the
remaining coloured paper roughly 1cm (⅜in) smaller than the first.

▲ step three

Cut one poppy seed head in half. Remove
the tops from three more. Discard the seeds.

◄ step four

Spray the larger rectangle of paper with glue and position centrally on the Perspex. Glue the second paper rectangle on top, then stick the poppies to the paper using the glue gun.

◄ step five

Paint the frame with your chosen base colour and leave to dry. Apply a generous coating of crackle glaze and again leave to dry.

TIP

Crackle glaze gives a lovely finish to your frame. Using a darker base coat and lighter top coat will achieve the most subtle effect as you will only see the darker colour in the cracks. It's worth experimenting and reversing the colours – although the effect is far less delicate it may suit a different style of work.

step six ►

Apply your chosen top colour and leave to dry. The paint will crackle giving an aged effect. For extra protection, finish with varnish or wax. Assemble the box frame (see pages 12–13).

floral bounty

Traditional crafts offer a range of items you can use to create displays. Silk flower buds, available from department stores or craft shops, add a three-dimensional element to this pretty boxed design, which is also embellished using flowers made with cake decorating tools.

materials and equipment

box frame (see method B, page 10)
fabric
scissors
graph paper
pen
approximately 20 silk flower buds
needle and coloured thread
aerosol glue
modelling material in two colours
rolling pin
sugar craft flower cutter
baking tray
emulsion paint in two colours
paintbrush
glue gun
frame glass cut to fit

◄ step one

Cut the backing board to size (see page 8). Cut a piece of fabric to fit the frame back plus an extra 1cm (⅜in) all round.

▲ step two

Place a piece of graph paper over the frame back. Cut this to size and mark out a pattern for the silk flower buds.

▲ step three

Lay the fabric over the graph paper and transfer your positioning marks on to the fabric.

◄ step four

Sew the silk flower buds on to the fabric where marked. Spray the backing board with aerosol glue and stick the fabric to the frame back.

◄ step five

Roll out one colour of modelling material to a depth of about 3mm (⅛in).

step six ►

Using the flower cutter make approximately 38 flower heads – you need enough to decorate the surround of your frame.

◄ step seven

Take tiny amounts of modelling material in the second colour and roll in your fingers to create tiny balls. Place these in the middle of the flower heads applying a little pressure to fix them in place. Put the flowers on a baking tray and bake in the oven according to the manufacturer's instructions.

TIP

Modelling material can be used to make a variety of three-dimensional objects with which to decorate your frames. Tiny shells could be used for a seaside theme or miniature tennis or footballs for a sporting collection.

step eight ►

Paint the box frame and frame surround in two matching shades and leave to dry. Glue the flowers on to the frame. Assemble the box frame (see pages 12–13).

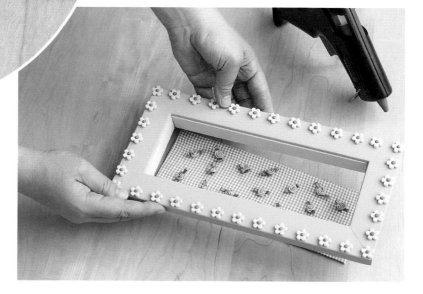

countrywide

Use delicate leaves to create a collection of colourful images. Displaying two or more frames makes a stylish work of art and you can vary the shape, size and finish of the frame according to the different types and colours of leaves you use.

materials and equipment

cold water fabric dyes

skeletal leaves

mountboard

ruler

chopping board

eyelet kit and hammer

brass rings

aerosol glue

box frame (see method A, pages 8–9)

glue gun or strong wood adhesive

handmade paper

pencil, bradawl and screw hooks

fine jewellery wire and scissors

paintbrush

frame glass cut to fit

▲ step one

Mix a fabric dye according to the manufacturer's instructions. Dip a leaf in the dye and leave to dry on newspaper.

▲ step two

Tear the mountboard into a rectangle making it 2cm (¾in) larger all round than the leaf.

step three ▶

Place the mountboard on a hard surface such as a chopping board. Using the eyelet kit, punch a hole in the middle of each side of the mountboard.

step four ▲

Insert an eyelet into each hole and fix in place using the eyelet tool and a hammer.

▲ step five

Fix a brass ring in each hole. Position the leaf centrally on the mountboard and stick in place using the aerosol glue.

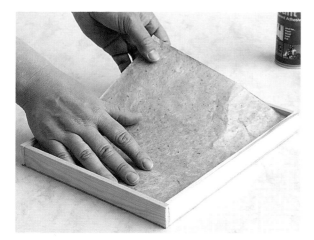

▲ step six

Glue the box frame to the frame back using a glue gun or strong wood adhesive. Cut a piece of handmade paper to fit inside the frame and glue in place using aerosol glue.

▲ step seven

Position the mountboard and leaf in the centre of the frame and mark the position of the rings on each side of the frame. Using a bradawl, make a small hole at each mark and then screw in the screw hooks.

TIP

You can also use dried leaves from the garden for this project or even cut leaf shapes from fabric and stick them to the backing board.

◄ step eight

Cut four lengths of jewellery wire and tie the wire through each brass ring. Then, stretching it taut, tie again through the hooks on the four sides of the frame.

◄ step nine

Stain the frame surround with fabric dye, allow to dry and assemble the box frame (see pages 12–13).

The variety in shape and size of natural objects means that they are the perfect choice when you want to experiment with unusual-shaped frames. From a long, thin flower, to a tiny seed head or a mixture of pebbles, each element calls for a different overall look.

simple seeds

Look around for shop-bought items that you can use in your box frame projects. A clear Perspex storage case is perfect for mounting little seed heads such as poppy seed heads, wheat ears and dried thistles, but could just as easily hold buttons or tiny toys. You can adapt the surround to suit the style of object and use a plain or coloured backing to match the items in the box. Stationery shops are a good place to look for unusual items. Also check out DIY shops and department stores.

faux flower

Fabric flowers, such as orchids, rosebuds and daisies, are now available in wonderfully realistic blooms. Where once designs were clearly fake, you can struggle now to distinguish them from the real thing. Perfect for framing, fabric flower heads offer colour and style inspiration. Create a classic picture with one beautiful bloom, a pretty natural paper backing and a stylish paint finish on the surround. A crackle-glaze is just one option and adds a touch of class to this special frame.

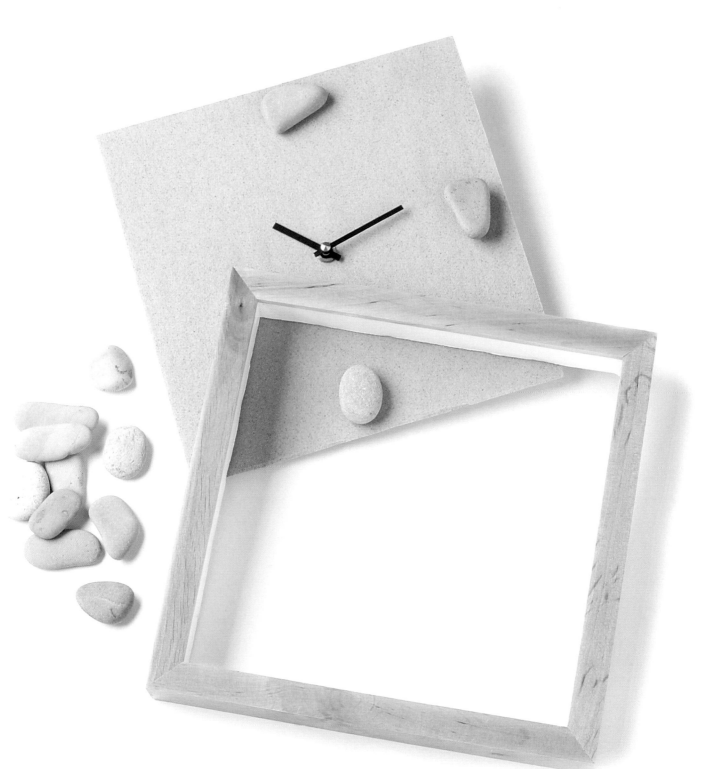

pebble clock

Play around with box frames and use them to create stylish accessories for your home. A collection of pebbles, a clock mechanism and chunky wood frame can be combined to make an original looking clock for the wall or mantelpiece. Battery-powered mechanisms are readily available from craft shops and mail order arts and crafts equipment suppliers. Keep things natural or use a coloured backing board and then paint the frame surround to match a specific colour scheme in your home.

family
occasions

A wedding, a birthday, a new home, a reunion or
even a birth – when you look at your calendar
over a year, there are countless occasions you
will want to remember. Mementos gathered at
the event make an ideal collection to put in a
box frame. Mix one-dimensional photos, tickets
or cards with three-dimensional memorabilia.
At a wedding, you should collect a champagne
cork, a flower and some confetti; if you are
celebrating the birth of a baby, a nappy pin or a
tiny bootie will be lovely in the frame and add to
the deeper quality of the overall image. Make
your memories from what you collect at these
special occasions.

Always be careful when you decide where to
display precious collections. If they are positioned
in bright sunlight they may fade and discolour
over time, so it is best to place them out of direct
sunlight in a slightly shadier spot.

holiday memories

While photographs in albums may sit on the shelf unopened, a framed display is always on show. Gather together bits and pieces from a holiday that you want to remember and use maps of the country and driftwood, if you spent time by the sea, to add the finishing decorative touches.

materials and equipment

travel map
aerosol glue
picture mount (see page 12)
scissors
paper glue
backing paper
box frame (see method B, page 10)
holiday memorabilia such as tickets, receipts,
 matchboxes and guides
acrylic paint in white, black and brown
paintbrush
driftwood
glue gun
frame glass cut to fit

◄ step one

Tear the travel map into strips
about 5cm (2in) wide and long
enough to overlap the width of
the picture mount.

step two ►

Spray the back of the strips
with aerosol glue.

▲ step three

Stick the map to the front
of the mount.

step four ►

Turn the mount over. Snip diagonal lines
into the inside corners of the picture mount
and fold and stick the map paper to the back.
Snip diagonal lines across the outside corners of
the mount and fold and stick the paper to the back.

step five ▶

Cut backing paper to fit the frame back and glue in place. Lay the picture mount on top of the frame back and arrange your holiday memorabilia inside until you are happy with the display. Remove the picture mount and glue the pieces in place.

TIP

Dry brushing is a simple technique used to add a little random colour. Simply take a tiny amount of paint on to a dry brush and brush on to the surface. Build up the effect very gradually. It's much easier to add colour a tiny bit at a time than to use too much and try and remove it.

◀ step six

Mix up a watery solution of acrylic paint – roughly two parts paint to one part water. You want to try and match the colour of your driftwood so use white and add a little brown or black until you get the right shade. Paint the frame surround.

step seven ▲

Dry brush touches of white and brown on to the frame surround to create a distressed effect.

◀ step eight

Using a glue gun, fix the driftwood to the frame surround. Assemble the frame (see pages 12–13).

wedding bells

Your wedding is a day to remember, and collecting memorabilia from the occasion provides plenty of material to make a wonderful framed display. This would make a treasured gift for a bride and groom, either straight after their big day, or to celebrate a first anniversary.

materials and equipment

box frame (see method B, page 10)
white emulsion paint
small paintbrush
wallpaper paste
strips of coloured tissue paper wide
  enough to overlap the frame
gold gilding wax
fabric
glue gun
scissors
coloured card
wedding memorabilia, such as confetti,
  ribbons, petals and the wedding
  order of service

◄ step one

Paint the frame surround with white emulsion paint.

▲ step two

Paint paste onto a section of the frame. Place the strips of tissue paper on top and work into the mouldings with the slightly gluey paintbrush.

TIP

For a coordinated look, identify a colour theme in the memorabilia and keep this in mind when choosing coloured tissue paper for the frame. For a personal touch, use a piece of the bride's or bridesmaid's dress material as the backing fabric.

▲ step three

Rip the edges of a small piece of tissue paper and place over the corner. Work it in with your fingers. Continue working around the frame, adding paste then working the paper into place with the brush. Leave the frame to dry for 2–4 hours.

◄ step four

Rub a little gilding wax on to your finger and work it along the edges of the frame. Keep a light touch – the overall effect should be heavier in some places than others.

▲ step five

Assemble the box frame and frame back (see pages 12–13). Cut fabric to the size of the frame back plus 2cm (¾in) all round. Using the glue gun, glue the fabric to the back and up the insides of the box frame.

▼ step seven

Position the memorabilia on the card and rearrange until you are happy with the overall image then glue in place.

TIP

Use paper glue to fix anything light into the frame, such as cards, telegrams and place names. Use a glue gun for any heavier items such as flowers, corks and wedding favours such as sugared almonds.

▲ step six

Cut coloured card to the size of the frame back minus 4cm (1¾in) all round. Position in the middle of the frame back and glue to the fabric.

▲ step eight

Assemble the box frame (see pages 12–13).

hello baby

Celebrate the birth of a baby with a decorative frame. Whether it's your own child or a baby born to family and friends, it's the perfect occasion for memory-making. Mixing memorabilia from the first few hours, days and weeks will make a wonderful display to treasure.

BOY OF HELEN
HAMMOND P262525

NOAH LOUIS HAMMOND

hello baby

materials and equipment

baby memorabilia, such as booties,
  nappy pins, congratulations card
  and hospital tag
various coloured papers
pencil and ruler
scissors
paper glue
box frame (see method B, page 10)
backing paper
glue gun
mosaic pieces
PVA (white) glue and small paintbrush
tile cutters and protective goggles
spatula or palette knife
tile grout
sponge
acrylic paint
frame glass cut to fit

▲ step one

Gather together cards and photographs and place them on top of the coloured paper. Draw around the objects, allowing a border of about 3mm (⅛in) all round. Cut out the coloured paper and glue the cards and photographs in place.

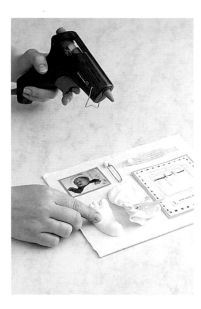

◄ step two

Cut some backing paper to fit the frame back and glue in place. Position baby mementos on the paper and rearrange until you are happy with the overall design then glue in place.

◄ step three

Assemble the frame surround and box frame (see pages 12–13). Fix whole mosaic pieces around the frame surround using PVA (white) glue.

step four ►

Once you have fixed the whole tiles use tile cutters to cut any extra bits to fit the gaps. It's important when you cut tiles to wear protective eye-wear. Goggles are available from any craft shop.

TIP

Making a cast of your baby's foot is simple. Silicone moulding material is non-toxic so simply press your baby's foot into the moulding material and then cast it in plaster.

◄ step five
Glue on the cut pieces of mosaic to fill the gaps.

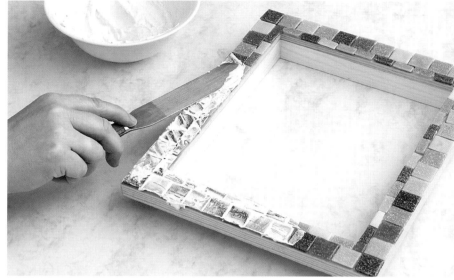

▲ step six
Using a spatula or palette knife, wipe the tile grout over the mosaic surface making sure it fills all the gaps.

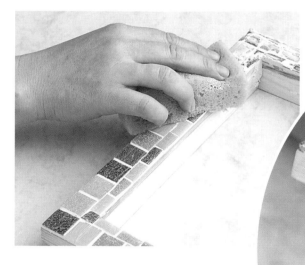

▲ step seven
Wipe over the surface of the tiles with a damp sponge to remove the excess grout.

step eight ►
Paint the edges of the frame surround and inside and outside the box frame and leave to dry. Assemble the box frame (see pages 12–13).

weekend break

It's amazing how much you can collect when you get away for a few days; postcards, coasters, and movie or music tickets all contribute to the collection. A short break may be appreciated all the more, so keep a special memento of the occasion.

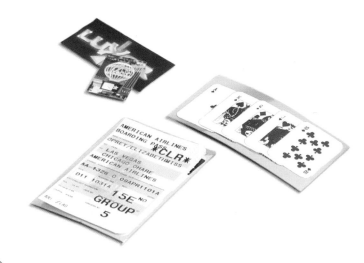

materials and equipment

box frame (see method D, page 11)
glue gun
coloured paper
ruler
pencil
craft knife
aerosol glue
holiday memorabilia, such as foreign
 coins, museum tickets, and restaurant
 and hotel business cards
paper glue
PVA (white) glue
paintbrush
aluminium foil
grate polish
absorbent paper
frame glass cut to fit

▲ step one

Attach the box frame to the frame back (see pages 12–13). Cut the coloured paper to fit inside the frame and stick in place using aerosol glue.

▲ step two

Position the holiday mementos on the paper and rearrange until you are happy with the overall design then glue in place.

▲ step three

Draw a design in pencil on the frame surround. Here, suits from playing cards and an abstract design reflect the theme of the weekend break, which was a trip to Las Vegas.

◄ step four

Go over your design with the glue gun, carefully tracing over each pencil mark. Allow to dry.

◄ step five
Cover the frame surround liberally
with PVA (white) glue.

◄ step six
Using long
strips of
aluminium foil,
wide enough
to overlap
the frame
surround, start
to cover the
surround.

◄ step seven
Work the aluminium foil into the
gaps and all around the design on
the frame surround. Overlap at the
corners and gently press any tears
together – these edges will be
camouflaged by the grate polish.

TIP
It's really important with this
technique that you work the foil
into every crevice. Take your time,
using the tips of your fingers to
achieve the best results. This will
take a while but it looks fantastic,
creating a three-dimensional
metallic effect on
your surround.

step eight ►
Dab some grate polish on to
absorbent paper and rub it over
the frame surround a section at a
time. Keep applying and rubbing
off until you achieve a pewter-like
finish. Assemble the box frame (see
pages 12–13).

Any event involving friends and family is a moment to remember. The beauty of box frames means that you can treasure the memories with a permanent reminder of the occasion.

happy valentines

Choose to surprise your sweetheart with a memento that will last long after cards have been put away. A red rose, decorative heart, miniature present and words of love can be gathered together to make a beautiful picture. Cover the frame with gold leaf for a sparkling finish.

moving home

Remember the old and record the new. A collection of luggage labels adorned with keys, pictures of your home and related items can be gathered together to make a memorable display.

family tree

Why not make a unique display table by simply adding legs to the base of a large box frame. Gather together photos of several generations of your family and arrange in the frame to create a fascinating family tree. You can write names and relationships on card beneath each picture to personalize it even more.

classic displays

Everyone collects something – from dolls' houses to teddy bears, from buttons to simple samplers – all of these items make an interesting exhibit. Remember that you can add extra colour to your finished frame by including an attractive picture mount or a colourful surround. This is where box frames make an impact. Your collection of brown bears can be brought to life with a vivid paint effect on the frame surround. A fabric sample that you have bought or created is given a stylish look with a similarly textured picture mount. Try out different looks.

A frame without a mount may work when the contents of the frame are visually strong. Adding a mount to the overall package creates a much more sophisticated and polished display.

home sweet home

Dolls' houses come in all shapes and sizes, and this open fronted box frame design makes a great alternative to more traditional options. The colours that you use should reflect the furniture that you choose, pine pieces with pretty wallpaper and a blue surround suit this modern design.

materials and equipment

box frame (see method A, pages 8–9)
ruler
pencil
craft knife
wood adhesive
masking tape
lengths of wood
saw
mitre saw
emulsion paint
paintbrush
wallpaper
cutting mat
wallpaper paste
scissors
dolls' house furniture

▲ step one

Cut the frame back, adding a triangle to one side to create a roof shape. Glue the box frame to the frame back and secure all round with masking tape. Leave for several hours to dry.

◄ step two

Measure the height and width of the inside of the box and cut three pieces of wood. One to fit across the middle and two shorter pieces to fit vertically above and below.

◄ step three

Use wood adhesive to fix the pieces in place.

TIP

Look for doll's house furniture in department stores, specialist shops and toy shops. Keep an eye out for unusual designs and then create your box frame around them. This box frame is ideal as a gift for a small child.

◄ step four

Measure the two sides of the triangular shape on the backing board and using a mitre saw, cut two more pieces of wood to make the roof sides adding an overhang of 1.25cm (½in) on each side.

step five ►

Using wood adhesive, fix the pieces in place.

◄ step six
Paint the inside and outside walls of the house.

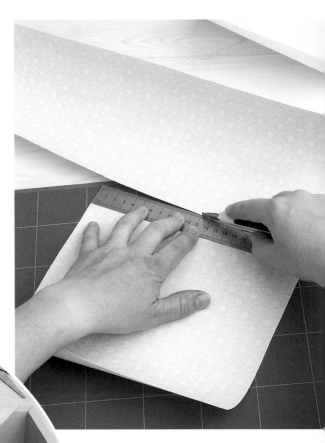

▲ step seven
Cut squares of wallpaper to fit roughly inside each room.

◄ step.eight
Position the wallpaper in the house to check that you are happy with the design.

◄ step nine

Paste the back of a piece of
paper and position it in a room.
Push firmly around the edge
scoring along the paper with
your fingernail. Pull the paper
out and then cut along the score
lines with scissors. Glue in place.

TIP

Pasting the paper and then
scoring the edges once you have
positioned it in each room gives
a much neater finish to your
wallpapering than trying to take
exact measurements and cutting
the paper while dry.

▼ step ten

Place the furniture in the house.

treasure trove

Create simple hanging shelves from a basic box frame and you can display well-loved objects around the home. Antique teddy bears are real collectibles and look perfectly at home in this stylish display. This would make a lovely feature in a child's bedroom.

treasure trove

materials and equipment

box frame (see method A, pages 8–9)
ruler
pencil
drill
emulsion paint
  in two contrasting colours
paintbrush
wax candle
medium sandpaper
rope or string

step one ▶
Measure and mark
two points on the top of the
box frame, about a third of the
way in from each edge.

◀ step two
Drill a hole at each
marked point.

TIP
This display uses the most
simple technique for making a
box frame and doesn't need a
frame back or surround –
so it's a great project for
a beginner.

▲ step three
Paint the box frame with emulsion,
inside and out, and leave to dry.

step four ▲
Rub the candle over the surface of the wood,
both inside the box frame and out, paying
particular attention to the edges and corners.

TIP

Adapt the shape and size of this project to suit the objects that you want to display. A collection of classic cars could be put in smaller frames and you could use wire to suspend them; single vases could be placed in individual frames then arranged in a group of three or four and hung from coloured ribbon.

▲ step five

Paint the box frame with your second colour and leave to dry.

◄ step six

Rub over the frame with sandpaper. Take time to work on the areas where you rubbed the most wax, the edges and corners. The idea is to give the frame an old-fashioned, worn appearance.

▼ step seven

Cut a piece of rope about 25cm (10in) long and thread one end through each hole. Tie each end in a chunky knot.

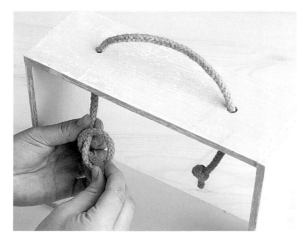

step eight ►

Arrange your teddy bears in the frame.

sewing matters

When you stitch your own samplers, sew decorative pieces of patchwork, or even collect swatches of unusual textiles, what is the best way to put them on display? A padded mount put in a simple frame makes the perfect backdrop for any fabric-based project.

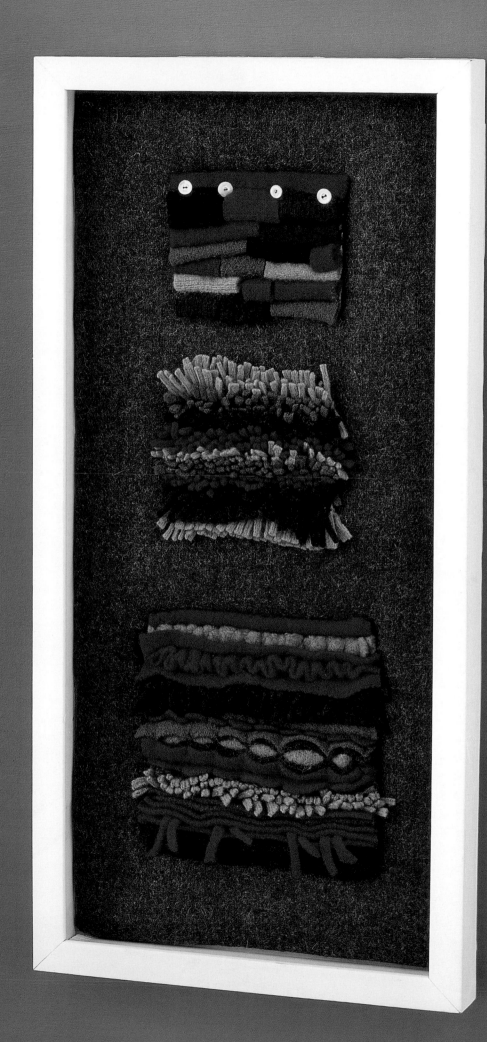

materials and equipment

card
box frame and backing board
  (see method B, page 10)
samplers
pencil
cutting mat
ruler
craft knife
wadding
scissors
upholstery adhesive
fabric
PVA (white) glue
emulsion paint
paintbrush

▲ step one

Cut the card to the same size as the frame back. Arrange the samplers on the card as you wish to display them and draw roughly around each one keeping as close to the edge of the fabric as possible.

◄ step two

Remove the samplers and draw accurate shapes about 3mm (⅛in) smaller than your original lines. Cut out the shapes.

TIP

Upholstery adhesive should be used in a well-ventilated space. Test it for suitability with samples of the materials to be used and protect the surrounding area from overspray. Allow 5–15 seconds until it's gone tacky before you apply the material.

step three ►

Cut pieces of wadding to fit the card and glue in place all the way round.

step four ▶

Place the card, wadding face down on your fabric and cut around the board allowing 2cm (¾in) all round. Glue the fabric to the wadding and the back of the card.

TIP

This display combines bold layers of felt and shrunk wool in toning colours. These were sewn together then cut, trimmed and worked into softly textured and very modern-looking samplers. A row of buttons along the top complete the look.

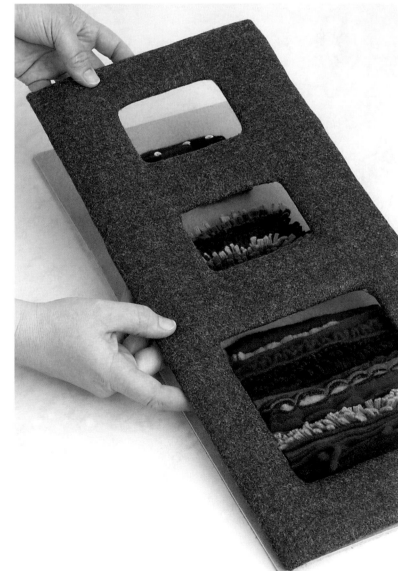

▲ step five

Cut two diagonal lines in the fabric across each window. Fold back each triangle and glue in place.

step six ▶

Glue your samplers to the frame back, making sure that they are positioned correctly for each window. Place the padded mount on top and ease the edges of the sampler through. Paint the box frame with white emulsion and leave to dry, then attach to the backing board (see pages 12–13).

simple style

Everyone has a button
box that accumulates
treasures over time.
Create a colourful display
by gathering together
the prettiest designs –
choose mother of pearl,
tortoiseshell and
translucent buttons and
you can make a unique
hanging display.

materials and equipment

box frame (see method B, page 10)
white paper
scissors and paper glue
sheer fabric
aerosol glue
coloured thread
selection of buttons
sticky tape
acrylic paint
paintbrush
size and sponge
silver leaf and soft brush
foam board
craft knife
picture mount (see page 12)
frame glass cut to fit

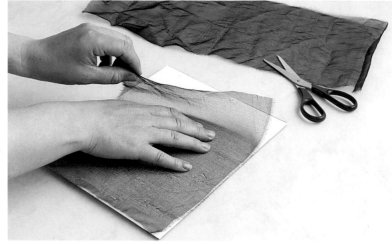

▲ step one

Cover the frame back with white paper and then sheer fabric cut to fit.

step two ▶

Cut six pieces of thread roughly twice the height of the frame. Thread the buttons on to the coloured thread.

step three ▲

Tie a knot behind each button to hold it in place. You will want about seven buttons on each piece of thread, depending on the size of your frame.

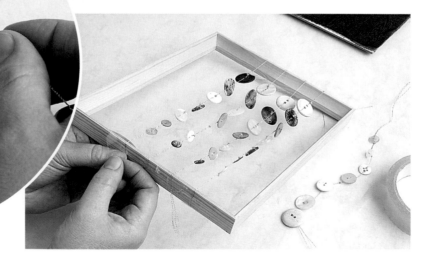

▲ step four

Using sticky tape, attach one end of each length of thread to the top of the box frame. Pull the thread taut and repeat at the other end. Trim the ends of the thread.

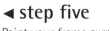

◄ step five
Paint your frame surround and leave it to dry.

step six ►
Dab size over the front of the frame surround. Using a sponge gives a mottled, rather than solid coverage.

TIP
Check when you are threading on your buttons that the top and bottom buttons on each length of thread will hang inside the picture mount when the frame is assembled. To do this, simply hold the mount in front of the box frame as you are threading on the buttons and again when sticking each length of thread in place.

◄ step seven
Apply silver leaf to the frame using a soft brush (a blusher brush is perfect for the job).

◄ step eight
To prevent the buttons banging against the glass, cut two pieces of foam board roughly 1cm (⅜in) wide to fit across the width of the picture mount. Glue in place at the top and bottom on the back of the mount.

step nine ►
Assemble the frame (see pages 12–13).

Once you start to develop projects you'll realize just how many items you have lying around the house that you can use in your frames. They may relate to a particular pastime or be something as simple as earrings.

earring storage

A simple box frame can be adapted to create a stylish place to keep earrings. Attach little hooks to the backing board and use tiny hinges to fix the front of the cupboard to the box. This would be perfect, too, for holding household keys.

anglers choice

A hobby may present you with items to put in your box frame and any fishing enthusiast will tell you that flies and lures offer a colourful display. When you are putting little items in a frame, it's important that they can be seen. Don't overdo the decoration around them and keep the backing board simple.

antique cutlery

Starting a collection of inexpensive but unusual and eye-catching items can be great fun. Rummage in antique markets and junk shops for old pieces of cutlery to put on display, then make a box frame to show them off. A verdigris paint finish on the frame complements the silver of the spoons.

making art

Have some fun with box frames – choose a design whether it is colourful or plain and add some entertaining elements. Art is appreciated on many different levels and what somebody loves, another person will hate – so indulge your own choices. Take sweets or collect postcards, think of flowers or a three-dimensional design that will work in your box frame. If your home is decorated with a neutral colour scheme, then maybe this is the opportunity to add a splash of colour. A boldly coloured frame will add interest to a plain wall and a bright collection of postcards – including all your favourite artists – will really stand out.

Check the lighting when you hang your frame. If the overhead light leaves areas of the room in shadow, you will want to move the picture into a brighter spot. Alternatively, placing it above a lamp may provide just the right amount of illumination and highlight your work.

picture this

Designing your own art display is simple, and much more fun than buying it straight from a gallery as you can customize it using your favourite painter's work. This clever display of postcards will impress even the most exacting of art critics.

WOLF KAHN

VINCENT VAN GOGH

picture this

materials and equipment

postcards
block of pine or wood offcut
pencil
ruler
saw
canvas
scissors
staple gun
white emulsion paint
paintbrush
printed names
embossing foil
masking tape
scribe or dry biro
box frame and backing board
  (see method B, page 10)
glue gun

▲ step one

Place a postcard on top of the wood block and draw around it adding a 3mm (⅛in) border. Cut this block out of the pine. Place on top of the canvas and cut around it adding a 3cm (1¼in) border all round. Repeat for the other two cards.

▲ step two

Staple gun the canvas to the back of each block of wood to create mini-mounting blocks.

step three ▶

Paint each canvas in white and leave to dry.

TIP

This box frame makes a great gift idea for someone you know who has a favourite artist or preferred school of art. Alternatively, gather together images of a favourite pop star or even photographs of a much-loved family pet and group together to create a montage of images. There is no need to glaze or use a frame surround for this style of frame.

WOLF KAHN

CLAUDE MONET

CLAUDE MONET

◀ step four

Place the printed name of one of the artists on top of the embossing foil. Secure it with masking tape and then trace over the letters using the scribe. Apply a reasonable amount of pressure to make sure that the words are embossed. Repeat with the names of the other two artists.

VINCENT VAN GOG

◄ step five

Cut out the name in an oblong shape and then reverse the embossing foil. Using a ruler and the scribe, draw a line all the way around the oblong about 1.5mm (¹⁄₁₆in) in from the edge. This is to create a framed effect and highlight the words. Repeat with the other two names.

▲ step six

Paint the frame back and box frame with white emulsion and leave to dry.

step seven ►

Glue a postcard to each block. Place the box frame on top of the frame back – for positioning purposes only – then glue the mounting blocks at equal distances on the backing board.

step eight ▶
Glue the nametags beneath the appropriate pictures.

TIP
Visit art galleries and you'll find hundreds of different images to choose from. Three cards by the same artists with the name of each painting added underneath works well. Alternatively type in the name of the artist repeatedly on your computer as running text and use the print out to cover the backing board. Keep the typeface tiny and you'll be amazed at how effective it can be.

◀ step nine
Glue the box frame to the frame back (see pages 12–13).

modern image

Simplicity itself, but so striking it will outshine even the most complex display. A mix of bold, colourful blocks and a grid of black lines drawn on a white background, in the style of abstract artist Mondrian, creates a vibrant look contained in a shiny silver frame.

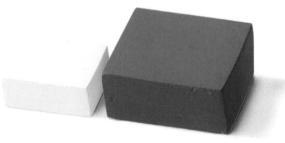

materials and equipment

box frame (see method B, page 10)
glue gun
white emulsion paint
paintbrush
several sheets of white cartridge paper
black pen
ruler
scissors
three pieces of wood, each a different thickness
pencil
saw
acrylic paint in three colours
silver aerosol paint

modern image

▲ step one

Glue the box frame to the frame back and leave to dry. Paint the whole piece with white emulsion and leave to dry.

step two ▶

Cut a template from white paper to fit into the frame back making it approximately 3cm (1¼in) smaller all round than the frame. Sketch out where you want to position your coloured blocks and label each square accordingly.

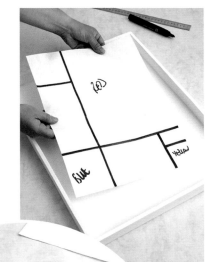

▲ step three

Carefully copy the grid on to white cartridge paper but do not write anything on the squares. Cut out the shapes marked with a colour from the original rough grid.

◀ step four

Place the cut out paper shapes on top of different pieces of wood and draw around them, then cut out the shapes using a saw. Using blocks of different thicknesses accentuates the three-dimensional effect of the finished piece.

◄ step five

Paint each wood block with the appropriate colour and leave to dry.

step six ►

Glue the cartridge paper grid to the frame back and then glue the painted wood blocks into the correct positions.

TIP

Whenever you use spray paint, make sure you work in a well-ventilated area (out of doors is ideal). If you wish to take extra precautions you can buy a small mask to cover your mouth from any DIY shop.

◄ step seven

Spray the frame surround with silver spray aerosol paint, leave to dry and then assemble the box frame (see pages 12–13).

candy art

Brightly coloured sweets are the starting point for this modern and very unusual piece. Keep a watch when you are working, though – it can take some time to fill the boxes if the family is on hand and help themselves before you finish!

materials and equipment

box frame and frame back
  (see method B, page 10)
undercoat
paintbrush
emulsion paint
clear plastic boxes
ruler
felt tip pen
scissors
white paper
aerosol glue
pencil
glue gun
sweets
picture corner brackets
bradawl
small screws and screwdriver
frame glass cut to fit

candy art

▲ step one

Undercoat the box frame and leave to dry. Paint the topcoat in a bright-coloured emulsion.

▲ step two

Measure the depth of the box frame and mark this on the plastic boxes.

step three ▲

Cut the boxes to this height. It's important to be accurate as the glass needs to sit tightly against the sweets to hold them in place.

TIP

Look in stationery shops for little clear plastic boxes. You will often find them filled with paper clips or drawing pins. Craft shops and DIY stores are also good sources of similar plastic containers.

step four ▶

Cover the backing board with white paper using aerosol glue. Position the boxes at equal distances down the frame back and mark the position for each one.

◄ step five

Using the glue gun stick the boxes to the backing board as marked.

TIP

For an eye-catching kitchen hanging, try filling boxes with dried herbs, spices and seeds with unusual shapes, such as star anise, dried pulses or colourful red lentils.

▲ step six

Fill each box with different sweets. A mix of brightly coloured ones and black and white sweets makes a striking combination.

◄ step seven

Assemble the frame using corner brackets to secure the glass to the front of the box frame (see pages 12–13).

fine design

Solitary flowers placed in single stem vases have taken over from more ornate floral arrangements. For a clever twist on this idea, try lining up test tubes in a frame and use the boldest of blooms, such as gerbaras, interspersed with simple foliage. Use roses to give a more traditional feel.

fine design

materials and equipment

test tubes
transparent outliner for glass
box frame (see method D, page 11)
primer
paintbrush
emulsion paint
saddle clips
silver aerosol paint
ruler
pencil
bradawl
screwdriver and screws

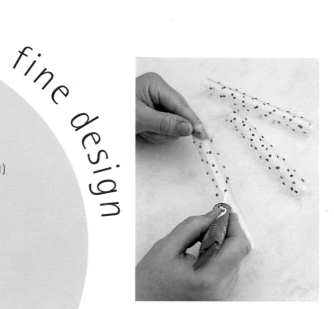

◄ step one

Put random dots of outliner on the glass test tubes and leave them to dry. Although it is called 'transparent' this product does have a colour to it.

step two ►

Paint the frame surround with primer and leave to dry. Finish with a topcoat of emulsion and leave to dry.

step three ►

Spray the saddle clips with silver aerosol paint suitable for use on metal, and leave to dry.

TIP

Keep in mind when you are positioning your test tubes that you need to be able to lift them out once the frame is assembled, in order to fill them with water. It's worth placing the box on top of the frame back and positioning the frame surround on top to check that this will be possible when you have assembled the frame.

◄ step four

Measure the width of the frame back, less the frame surround, and position the test tubes at equal distances across the board. Mark the position of each one. Remember that they are going to hold a flower so they need to be closer to the bottom of the frame than the top, to allow for the flower heads.

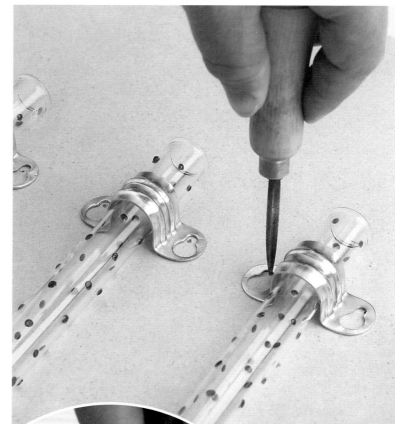

◄ step five
Place the saddle clips over the tubes, while they are in place, and mark the position of the screws.

step six ►
Using a bradawl, make a hole where each screw is to go. You need these marks as you will be putting in the screws after you have sprayed the backing board so you will not be able to see any pencil marks.

▲ step seven
Spray the frame back and box frame with the silver aerosol paint and leave to dry.

◄ step eight
Screw the saddle clips into position on the frame back and assemble the box frame (see pages 12-13). Fill each test tube with water and carefully reinsert into the clips before putting a flower into each one.

Creating frames that you can display as art gives you scope to mix and match almost anything. Choose colours with care and focus on one particular theme whether it be a favourite film star, a collection of tools and materials or even tiny toys.

artist's palette

The tools of a trade can be used to create an unusual display – and would be the perfect gift for someone with a related job or hobby. Many people relax by painting, and a palette and oil paints complete with brushes looks like a modern work of art when gathered together and framed.

movie star

Favourite pictures and related mementos are a great way of displaying items that might otherwise just sit in a drawer. A collection of photos, magnets, stickers and a clapper board all celebrate the life and work of Audrey Hepburn, and make a fittingly stylish display. You might choose similar items relating to a musician and include violin strings and sheet music or a miniature football or replica kit to accompany a sports star.

antique art

An old font case (used to hold letters in years gone by, when printers typeset each word individually) offers a ready-made and segmented frame. Tiny toys – the type you'll find inside chocolate eggs or given away free from hamburger restaurants – make a bright and modern display when placed inside each individual section.

suppliers

Most materials required are available from picture framers, do-it-yourself shops and art suppliers. Alternatively, make a search on the Internet under picture frame supplies and you will find thousands of companies that can supply all the kit for your projects. The following list includes some specialist companies.

UK

ART SUPPLIES

Cowling and Wilcox
26-28 Broadwick Street
London W1F 8HX
tel: 020 7734 9557
www.cowlingandwilcox.com

Falkiner Fine Papers
76 Southampton Row
London WC1B 4AR
tel: 020 7831 1151

T N Lawrence
208 Portland Road
Hove
East Sussex BN3 5QT
tel: 01273 260260

London Graphic Centre
2 Western Avenue Business Park
Mansfield Road
London W3 0BZ
tel: 020 8969 6644

Paperchase
213-215 Tottenham Court Road
London W1P 9PF
tel: 020 7467 6200

E Ploton (Sundries) Ltd
273 Archway Road
London N6 5AA
tel: 020 8348 2838

Stewart Stevenson
68 Clerkenwell Road
London EC1M 5QA
tel: 020 7253 1693

SPECIALIST PAINTS

Annie Sloan
117 London Road
Headington
Oxford OX3 9HZ
tel: 0870 6010082
www.anniesloan.com

Craig and Rose
Unit 17
Stewart Fields
New Haven Road
Edinburgh EH6 5RQ
tel: 0131 5553773

Fired Earth
Twyford Mill
Oxford Road
Adderbury
Oxfordshire OX17 3HP
tel: 01295 812088
www.firedearth.com

Plasti-Kote Ltd
London Road Industrial Estate
Pampisford
Cambridge CB2 4XP
tel: 01223 836400

CRAFT SUPPLIES AND SUNDRIES

The Dolls House Emporium
High Holborn Road, Ripley
Derbyshire DE5 3YD
tel: 01773 513773
www.dollshouse.com

Dylon International Ltd
Worsley Bridge Road
Lower Sydenham
London SE26 5HD
tel: 020 8663 4801

Fred Aldous Ltd
37 Lever Street
Manchester M1 1LW
tel: 0161 2362477

Homecrafts Direct
PO Box 38
Leicester LE1 9BU
tel: 0116 2697733
www.homecrafts.co.uk

Pebeo
Unit 109
Solent Business Centre
Millbrooke Road West
Millbrooke
Southampton SO15 0HW
tel: 02380 701144

Russell & Chapple
68 Drury Lane
London WC2B 5SP
tel: 020 7836 7521

US

Dick Blick Art Materials
PO Box 1267
Galesburg
IL 61402-1267
tel: 800 828 4548
www.dickblick.com

Graphik Dimensions Ltd.
2103 Brentwood Street
PO Box 10002
High Point NC 27263
tel: 800 332 8884
www.pictureframes.com

The Home Depot
2455 Paces Ferry Road
Atlanta, GA 30339-4024
tel: 770 433-8211
www.homedepot.com

The Professional Picture Framers Association (PPFA),
4305 Sarellen Road
Richmond
Virginia 23231
tel: 800 556 6228 or 804 226 0430
www.ppfa.com

Wits End Mosaic
5028 S Ash Avenue Ste 104
Tempe, AZ 85282
tel: 480 456 0364
www.mosaic-witsend.com

the author

Lizzie O'Prey has over fifteen years experience as a writer, stylist and art director. She currently works as a freelance writer and editor in the fields of home decorating, interior design and creative crafts. She is based in North London and has worked for a number of leading magazines including *Inspirations For Your Home*, *House Beautiful*, *Home* and *Perfect Home*. When not writing she spends time renovating her Victorian terraced house and walking Sam the black labrador. Contact Lizzie at www.lizzieoprey.com

the crafter

Helen Atkinson studied 3D Design and Ceramics at art college and since then has gone on to make her name in the field of interior design, creative crafts and paint effects. She has appeared as a designer on several television programmes including BBC's *Real Rooms* and contributes regularly as a maker, journalist and stylist for many of the leading home-interest magazines. She lives and works in South East London.

acknowledgments

With thanks to Stewart Grant for his enduring patience and skill with a digital camera and to Mike Bracken and Tim Hammond for their unceasing support.

index

Page numbers in **bold** refer
to project titles

aluminium foil 54–5
Angler's Choice **78**
Antique Art **101**
Antique Cutlery **79**
Artist's Palette **100**

baby mementoes 48--51
backing board 6
berries 17
boxes, clear 36, 94
box frame, making 8–15
buttons 74–7

cake decorating equipment
   28–31
Candy Art **92–5**
chillies 18–23
clocks 37
collage 72
collectibles 58–79
corner brackets 94–5
Countrywide **32–5**
crackle glaze 15, 26–7, 36
cutlery 79

dolls' house 60–5
driftwood 40–3
dry brushing 43
dyes 14, 34–5

Earring Storage **78**
embossing foil 82–7
embroidery 72
equipment 7
eyelets 34

Family Tree **57**
Faux Flower **36**
feathers 17
Fine Design **96–9**
fishing flies 78
Floral Bounty **28–31**

flowers 17
   silk 28–31, 36
   test tube vases 96–9
foam board 77
font case 101
footballs 31
frame back 8–11
frame size 17
frame surround 8–11
Fresh and Wild **18–23**
fruit 18–23

Garden Source **24–7**
gilding wax 46
glass 6
   corner brackets 95
   fitting frame with 13, 23
   rebated surround 13
   transparent outliner 98
glue gun 7, 43–4
gold leaf 15, 56
grate polish 54–5
grouping frames 17, 32

handmade paper 26–7, 34–5
hanging rope 68–9
Hello Baby **48–51**
Holiday Memories **40–3**
Home Sweet Home **60–5**

keys 78
kitchens 18–23

leaves 17, 32–5
lighting 81

maps 40–3
materials 6
memorabilia 39–57
metallic paint 15, 91, 98–9
modelling material 30–1
Modern Image **88–91**
Mondrian, Piet 88
mosaic 48–51
mouldings, wood 6

mountboard 6
mounts 59
   covering 42
   cutting 12
   padded 70–3
Movie Star **100**
Moving Home **56**

paint
   crackle glaze 15, 27, 36
   distressing 15, 68–9
   dry brushing 43
   finishes 14–15
   metallic 15, 91, 98–9
   spray aerosol 91
patchwork 70
Pebble Clock **37**
Perspex 6, 26–7
pets 85
Picture This **82–7**
plaster casts 20–3, 48–51
poppy heads 24–7, 36
postcards 82–7

saddle clips 98–9
safety 7
samplers 70–3
seed heads 17, 24–7, 36–7
Sewing Matters **70–3**
shells 17, 31, 40–3
silicone moulding paste
   20–3, 50
silk flowers 28–31, 36
silver leaf 15, 76–7
silver paint 91, 98–9
Simple Seeds **36**
Simple Style **74–7**
sporting themes 31
star anise 24, 36
strawberries 23
suppliers 102
sweets 92–5

teddy bears 66–9
tennis balls 31

test tube vases 96–9
textiles 28–31, 70–3
thistles, dried 36
tissue paper 46
toys 69, 101
transparent outliner 98
Treasure Trove **66–9**

Valentine **56**
varnish 14
vases 69, 96–9
vegetables 18–23
verdigris paint 79

wallpaper 64–5
wax candle 15, 68–9
Wedding Bells **44–7**
Weekend Break **52–5**
wheat ears 36
wire 6, 34–5
wood stain 14, 22